COPYRIGHT

Editing and Layout by Amina Chitembo.
Cover Designed by Ahsan Chuhadry.
Cover Artwork by Vivian Timothy.
Published by Diverse Cultures Publishing, UK.

Website: www.diverse-cultures.co.uk

Email: publishing@diverse-cultures.co.uk

ISBN: 978-1-9160114-4-1

DEDICATION

To my Husband Hagen and my daughter Shanaya. This two people keep me grounded and wake me up to conquer the world and achieve my dreams.

CONTENTS

"There is nothing that has not been said. I will join others to put things in words and writings to better fate and inspire souls: If you are a part of this weariness, you are my target, so join and never be singled out."

PROLOGUE

We all are veiled, covered and wearied with pains of our roots. We have been robbed of our roots and are left to float without embedding and anchoring properly. Though many can no longer complain, and no longer have enough tears, to weep for a lost and uprooted root, and the souls in chains, and the bleeding hearts and broken hearts.

We can be tired with other things, we can make do with other things that life bestowed on us, but we cannot manage our weary states, and broken minds when we lose our roots, we just looked like we battled with the world and the world had won the battle.

We are in pains and chains, we are lost, and waiting to be found by those whom we entrusted power on. When they lose their vision to lead well, we cease to be their focus, and we suffer, perish and lose our anchor.

Consider a tree whose roots are shaken when a whirlwind set in, whose roots get uprooted because it is no longer strong enough to withstand the force of the winds, whose anchor is destroyed when no protection or remedy is at hand, what follows is a thin feeling. The root of all trees, serve a stronghold and is where all good things originate.

Joyce Meyer once wrote 'Consider a tree for a moment. As beautiful as trees are to look at, we don't see what goes on underground – as they grow roots. Trees must develop deep roots to grow strong and produce their beauty. But we don't see the roots, we just see and enjoy the beauty. In all, we must do everything to preserve, protect and guard our roots, for once damaged, tampered with, takes decades to repair possibly and may not be the same again.

When we get lost elsewhere, our roots give us the comfort, the feelings that we belong, and we feel at home. Back to our root is where love is in abundance, but what happens when the roots are uprooted by those who were supposed to care for them? Uuups! Our anchor gets tampered with, and that which hold us is no longer able to hold us forever.

> *"I would go to the deeps a hundred times to cheer a downcast spirit. It is good for me to have been afflicted, that I might know how to speak a word in season to one that is weary."*
>
> - Charles Spurgeon-

OUR PAINS

A way of dealing with the pains and the long-awaited 2019 Nigerian elections. This book says it all. When our roots are destroyed, where else can we call home! The importance of one's root is reaped into pieces. When we get lost elsewhere, our root gives us the hope 'the anchor and the feelings of being wanted again.

This is the 21st century and Nigerians once more hope for a saviour for the next four years. While other countries have achieved democracy without manipulation, killings, and destruction, in Nigeria, no election passes by without Nigerians, home and abroad having to go through pains of the chains of political enslavement, sleeplessness and thoughts of what will happen next! Gripped with fear, pain, chains and yet, locked and imprisoned by our roots.

Our root, our pain and the possibilities of attaining a democracy without loss of lives and properties remain a dream for me as a Nigerian writing this book, watching from a foreign land while still a patriot of my Country.

OUR FEARS

Undoubtedly, our weariness is not based on the fact that we are running. Rather, our weariness is all too frequently based on the fact that many of the things that we are running from are the very things we should be running to- Craig D. Lounsbrough.

The nearer the Nigerian 2019 election drew closer, the more panic I am. Are we truly running away from those very things we should turn to? I must confess that I went through agony, pains and doubts during the just concluded Nigerian election. Since I did not know what do to, I decided to deal with the pains, the agony and the frustrations of the 2019 Nigerian election through writing.

I am so passionate about writing because it has helped me deal with the darkest moments of my life, even most uncertainties of life, that I felt there was no way out.

I intend that many readings will know that I am not a politician, and do not attach myself to any political party. I have been so hopeful of my country that things were going to change soon for better until I realised how bad the situation way back home is. I am not just talking about anything; I am talking about my beloved country, Nigeria. Our country needs help, not from the outside world, rather from all Nigerians for we are the ones to revive our own country.

There are so many reasons why distractions should be ignored at this point. Why blame games should be over, and why we should be more realistic and not emotional in dealing with issues of national matters.

Our kids are watching, and even some are wondering 'what a confused nation' — and questioning what may be going on.

Is that what we are going to hand over to our kids?

This book is written in honour of our many African brothers, sisters and children especially to the many Nigerians who lost their lives in civil war, terror attacks, gotten displaced, died on the way to Libya, drowned in the Mediterranean Sea in the course of seeking for a better life , and especially for my "IMO STATE" that suffered negligence in the past years.

For the veiled, the heart-broken, trodden, for the tribes that have been beaten, killed and rejected and made strangers in their land due to injustice.

To you and to many that died in the just concluded Nigerian election of 2019, all is not lost there is hope, hope of rebirth, liberation, hope of getting to the promised land, and hope that one day justice shall resurrect for those who have been marginalised, forgotten and have suffered injustices in their land.

Someday, sometime, we shall all wake up to realise that after all, we all are one, from same flesh, and same soul with one God that has different names for everyone.

It is only when we become our 'Brothers keepers ' that we will then start to appreciate one another, then we will begin a new chapter that will be inclusive and not exclusive, tolerant and not tribalistic nor ethnocentric, Religious battle, terror attacks, intimidation, kidnappings, and other crimes against humanity will vanish and disappear.

We will speak in one voice despite having different accents; we will love one another not minding our indifferences and short-comings, we will not kill, not judge and not condemn others. We will learn and accept the others in us; after all, we all originated from one being.

No more, no less- 'We are tired, and we want our homes made homes again, and not homes made pains' and thorns. Selfishness, greediness, must stop, and leaders must be leaders again. Sentiments have nothing in common with leadership. Instead, integrity, leading by a good example, and sacrificing are all it requires to lead well.

To my knowledge, marginalised people, unemployed youths, bad roads, lack of Infrastructure and others are signs of a nation in distress. Is this not reason enough to collectively do things together for the good of our nation.

You may be wondering why I am getting extremely so worried about my root. I am trying not to be depressed and not to show my sadness, but the fact is that this is my root and no matter how hard I try not to think about it, its memories still find their way in.

Is my country Nigeria truly in distress, or are we just pretending that all is well?

I read the article of Samuel Adesanya online written 12months ago, confirming that Nigeria is in distress- He pointed out some of the very common things that have distressed Nigeria. In all these, one could have wondered, what lessons the entire nation may have learnt from the past mishaps?

Laws and rules are meant for everyone, as the Constitution should protect freedom and belief, as well as the freedom to worship. In America and most Western worlds, people seem to be more protected by the constitution; this is far from reality in Nigeria.

I know this sounds familiar. We all love peace and work so hard to live in peace, and not to live in fear. I extend my wish, my hope and my dreams that we all will witness a new and positive change in Nigeria; it is truly my hope that every Nigerian follow suit to get Nigeria working again.

All it takes is a few good dedicated citizens to wriggle out of corruption and turn things going.

We are not' shit holes, as trump described Africa, we are not shit holes, we have all it takes to debunk this but are we ready?

All People in Nigeria are tired of living in compromise, in sorrow, and are tired of wanting more and getting less and getting out of wanting because of the crumbled system.

It is my hope and my wish, and they wish of many that we stop this war and make peace, that we live and let live, for we are a continent of hope and not doom, a state for all, facing a common giant.

I found this very helpful, and I trust God will renew our energy.

"God renew our energy when we are tired"

- Psalm 103:5.

We are truly tired, tired of all that is not going right,
Tired because resources are wasted, stolen and unequally shared,
Tired because of our shortcomings,
Tired because of our collective failure,
Tired because we are not sure who to believe,
And who to give the mantle of leadership to,
And who we can call our Joseph, our Moses, our Aaron, our Daniel.
Who can fight our Giant Goliath?
And rule in Solomon's wisdom?
Who, and who can do that for us?
Oh! God renew our energy, our hopes,
And restore our roots.
It does not matter who becomes the leader, what matters is who cares for the people's needs

For faithfulness and love of the people is what people look for in a leader, they prefer a poor good leader and not a rich bad leader, without a heart.

Africa, my beautiful continent, blessed with all, including natural resources, manpower and beauty. Black is beautiful and unique. Unfortunately, other continents appreciate and know what Africa has except the black people, this is sad, because as long as we are not able to cherish and care for what we have, the wish to make Africa great again may continue to elude us.

Africa is said to be the second world largest and most populous continent, being behind Asia in both categories (Wikipedia). It is surrounded by the Mediterranean Sea to the north, Red Sea to the northeast, the Indian Ocean to the Southeast and the Atlantic to the West. Has about fifty-four countries, nine territories, Majority of the continent and its countries said to be in the Northern hemisphere, many in the southern.

Algeria said to be Africa's largest and Nigeria has the highest population. Eastern Africa is seen as the origin of human beings. Nigeria has the largest ethnicities, cultures and languages.

According to history, Africa was colonised by Europe in the 19th century, decolonised in the

20th century. Nigeria, like other African countries, is a member of African Union (AU), with its headquarters in Addis Ababa.

The question that everyone kept asking Why are most African countries poor despite its numerous natural resources, and why is Nigeria amidst of her great natural and human resources still struggling, what is wrong, are we a continent of struggle, doom or cursed!

Only 15 countries are reported to qualify as the 'mineral-rich', of which Nigeria is one in West Africa. Still, everything is wrong except with Botswana that can at least boast of being stable. Is that the story we should be telling ourselves in this 21st century?

Daron Acemoglu and James Robinson in Why African nations fail, clearly stated in their article that Africa has not developed because the leaders in charge do not understand the business. The leaders have reportedly failed to invest in the POWER OF THE PEOPLE, and this is a big problem.

Why, why my Africa?

Is this really the case as reported?

I am sure that many of us know this is some part of our problems until today. This must change, and we have to start believing in ourselves again, to use what we have to get what we want.

There is power, knowledge and wisdom in our people, but we have to discover and start appreciating what we have.

Some of the African countries like Nigeria blessed with natural resources are blinded by minerals as if only the mineral resources can do the magic, hardly can Nigeria boast of being able to transform their natural resources to finish product, except with the help of the western world. Who after they have finish refining the products in any form will, in turn, sell it back to us? They make their gains, and we make our loss.

Sad, really sad.

CHAPTER 1: OUR NIGERIA

Geographically Nigeria is in West Africa and shares borders with Niger in the North, Chad in the northeast, Cameroon in the east, and Benin in the West.

Made up of 36 states and one federal territory, theoretically democratic Flag is Green white green.

Motto: Unity and Faith, peace and progress

Anthem: Arise O Compatriots.

Major languages are Igbo, Hausa, and Yoruba with many other dialects. Lagos is the largest city, the former capital before it was moved to Abuja.

History has it that Nigeria is a home for many ancient kingdoms and traditions. They had an existing system before the colonial rule, call it anything but this is what we were told of our Land.

According to history, Nigeria was not supposed to be one country, but our British colonial rulers, felt it was good for them to manage then in the 19th century, not minding the differences in culture, language, these have led to a lot of conflicts that have plagued the nation till today. History was one of my best subjects and am glad I took it as a subject in secondary school, where we learnt so much about colonial rules then that divided Nigeria into, the southern Nigeria protectorate and northern Nigeria protectorate in 1914.

Yes, they even came as missionaries, brought religion to us. Yes, religion is beautiful only when we get spiritually involved, but are we spiritually involved!

History thought us about the Indirect rules of our British colonial master which when judged today did not lead us to anywhere, rather Nigeria has been known in history to have faced a series of coup, religious conflicts, marginalization of some groups and imbalance in power distribution and allocation of federal resources this has set Nigeria backward till today.

Nigeria is popularly known as the 'Giant of Africa' because of its largest population, which is estimated to be 186 million. It is said to be the 7th most populous in the world, with 3rd largest youth. It is estimated to have about 250 ethnic groups, with 250 different languages, and different cultures.

English is the official language, due to the British colonial rules then-, Pidgin English is also accepted but not at the academic level. Yes, the colonial master made us believe that everything black was not good enough, and some of us believed, and we try to imitate the style of their dressings while neglecting our beautiful and natural ways of doing things. The irony is that they still use our stuff to make wrappers and in turn sell them to us; the classical example is 'Hollandia's very popular stuff for Nigerian women, used in ceremonies. This prestigious industry is run and owned by a European, what an irony. No wonder we became careless with most things we were endowed with. We used to be natural people, today we are not anymore, rather we are confused than ever, unless we decide to go back to our roots, and do our natural things, and believe in the powers we have to improve and develop our things. It still will remain a long way to discovering what we have.

Nigeria has Christians mostly in the South and Muslims in the North. In the past, both religions co-existed peacefully. I have so many friends who are Muslim, and we celebrated with each other. Today we have both Christian and Muslims fanatics in Nigeria, and this is destabilising the nation, because of the confusing states we suddenly found ourselves in. We believe in the almighty above, and hope He brings and restores our uprooted roots.

A country that is seen as the 20th largest economy. A member of African Union (AU), MINT group referring to the economies finances of Mexico, Indonesia, Nigeria and Turkey, Nigeria is also a member of United Nations, Commonwealth nations and OPEC (Organisation of the Petroleum Exporting Countries) a-14-nations organisation founded in 1960, and yet everything is not going well, despite having all and belonging to big organisations.

Are we so confused? Have we lost all the ability to believe in ourselves? And do the right things?

Why is everything going wrong?

Daron and James Robinson in Why African Nations fail a book supposed to be a synopsis of all the various theories and studies, see all peculiar problems in most African countries. Imagine having tons of raw coffee, having barrels of crude oil and exporting to the Western world, they finish the products, refine our gas and oil and import to us, all due to failure to understand business. In so doing, the Africans lose, and the West make money, they are right in their analysis, and this must change if we hope to achieve a better Africa, especially a better Nigeria.

This belief of having mineral resources have doomed us for life. From every indication, it is this same attitude that has produced Government, and citizens that have depended more on foreign help in processing the mineral resources, who in turn take the real money and give Africans peanut. They remain rich, more industrialised, and we remain poor and underdeveloped.

People are getting greedy and are believing in making fast money without that kind of work that goes with it, crime and of course all that goes with it are becoming the orders and normal practice. Corruption is eating up every corner. We all are getting greedy every day, and this is resulting to corruption and conflict everywhere, see Nigeria, Sierra Leone, Republic of Congo and many more, all because we have surrendered and have lost the ability to do the right thing, and task ourselves. Are we going to go on give the Western world all the credit, and depend on finished goods from the West? We can do better, all we need do is to start using our various gifts and talents to redefine things.

Bad leadership kills a nation: Poor governance has led most nations to more conflict, strife and disorder. Intimidations of the poor by the rich is seen as normal, unexplored natural resources, lack of investment in education, health, social capital becomes norms. Nearly everything remained poorly developed, and people suffer. We go about to boast that we have natural resources, and we are giant of Africa, yet we are in pains and chains.

Nigerians believed too much in oil and gas and having the feeling of a rich son that can afford all with merely knowing that his father has oil. Handiworks are not attractive in any form, even though these class of profession sustains a nation. Sometimes, more emphasis is laid on university graduates, don't get me wrong, having lived in Germany, and having seen that Germany after the war got rebuilt again, with mere coal and human knowledge, don't tell me we can't do more than that, we have natural resources and we have human resources, so what do we lack? . We lack natural and sincere people; we lack people who believe in us, who are ready to use what they have to make Nigeria great again. We have believed too much in all except believing in us. We are choosing our priority wrongly, and we are failing our nation. Some who after graduating in languages like Igbo, Yoruba, Hausa go into work as a banker, this is a problematic sign.

Countries that have believed they are rich by mere mentioning that they have mineral resources, and cannot transform what they have, and have rather resorted into not thinking, which ways to get at end positive result with what they have. We can do more and better. Corruption, which has misled leaders and citizens and has cut us all off and has blinded our vision can be curbed, but we have to do things together for the good of our nation collectively.

Botswana has proven different compared to other African countries.

What is gas and oil to Nigeria If our people keep on suffering?

Is this a curse or a blessing?

OUR PEOPLE

They cry aloud, but no one hears, what is a nation without its youth, and its citizens?

Why is a nation so rich and endowed with natural resources, and at the same time very poor and insecure?

According to Wikipedia's definitions, Mineral resources are materials of economic interest found in or on the earth's crust in such quality, quantity and form that could be used for economic extractions. Mineral resources sustain the economy of those nations that have them.

Yes, Nigeria has all it takes to feed its wards and make a good life for all, rather we have chosen to make some rich while so many are left begging for a day's meal.

Nigeria possesses Petroleum and Natural gas, this was discovered in 1959, coal (1909) at Enugu, Bitumen, Iron ore, Gypsum, Gold, Talc, Lead and Zinc, Sunlight, Fertile land, all are resources meant to be refined sold and reinvested in the economy.

Unfortunately, since independence in 1960, Nigeria has faced a series of coups, the civil war in 1967 that lasted for three years. This set Nigeria a decade backward, but did we learn anything from history? Looking at how things are, one will just be exclaimed and say, not very likely.

It is known that 1979 born a new constitution, but how far are we protected? Are we plagued and cursed with bad leaders! This plague continued with coups, corrupt and misfortunes that have set Nigeria another decade backwards. We all are in the same boat, crying for our beloved country, hoping upon hopes for a great country for our future generation.

We are blessed with so much, but for some reasons, we are restricted and used only Petroleum and other natural gases, discovered in Oloibiri, Bayelsa, in 1959 as the only source of revenue. Reportedly, 2.5 million barrels of crude oil said to be produced per day; the gas reserve is said to be put at 160 trillion cubic meters. Don't forget Nigeria is a member of OPEC.

Eight states are known as oil producing, namely; Niger Delta, Akwa Ibom, Ondo, Abia, and Imo State, many states are being discovered recently.

What happened to our resources? And why are things looking so bad for all of us?

We are giant of Africa with four refineries, that could process and finish our oil products, yet this is not the case, we continue to suffer from this huge challenge.

Yes, we have four refineries!

What is more, what went wrong?

All of the refineries are non-functioning. How about the two in River States; in Warri, and Kaduna?

Mmhhhh! One will say we are truly in distress.

Consequently, who can our David be?

These questions kept recurring to me. I had battled with this thought just like every other Nigerian.

But the thoughts and torments became worse during the elections 2019. My heart would make plans, try to think out and imagine a beautiful Nigeria.

I would Draw plans in my head of how I would want my beloved country to look like,

Yes, I dreamt dreams that coloured my world with beautiful rainbow colours. How I wanted my country Nigeria to look like.

I see my dream country, Imagined as I walked down the corner where we lived. The questions came up again and again in my mind;

And I ask myself, why are we not making any progress?

Anyway, why are my still having sleepless nights and panic when I call home and think of home?

Why have we remained stagnant in all spheres?

Are we really stuck, stacked and stagnant?

Nigeria has mineral resources everywhere, hidden and buried, and yet, we are not getting completely out of our chains.

In all the 56 states of Africa, I would have bet for anything, to have a dreamland and fields of riches. I do not know how you fight and struggle with your loneliness and pains of your roots,

I am fighting my pains with my writing,

How about you, how does it look like to fight disappointment?

How does it look like to fight dashed hopes?

Where is the hope, the struggle and beliefs we have known from our forefathers?

We believe should have carried us all through.

Even in the face of worries. And bad governance

How smoothly it would have been for all of us children of Africa rich and poor, to behold our beloved land.

How beautiful we would have spoken,

And recite our hymns,

And praise our heads,

I lost sleep, and had headache,

Thinking what we all can do to restore our sinking country,

I lost my heart,

and lost my strength,

Wondered even in daylight.

I repeated this question over and over again in my head

As I sought answers for me,
I despair, and I cry for my country,
My country in despair.
I shall never expect an answer so soon,
But I shall never fail to remind myself daily,
That God still has plans for us,
I cast my cares and worries in God
I do not doubt that God will deliver us.
Anytime soon!

Nigeria has so many unexplored resources. We buy from other countries instead of exploring what they have on our home soil. I find it difficult to understand; I do not know about you. We are all to blame for the demise and diminishing country that could be so rich. More so the politicians and the rich of our motherland.

These thoughts and questions are my way of dealing with the election saga

Have we not learnt wisdom?

Do you know what we are doing wrong?

We are doing our motherland wrong. We are painting our soil red. In the wake of another election, the weak suffer, the few honest are hated, and the truth blurred, subdued.

We all listen to false preachers,

The oppressed are merged with the poor, and vision is blindfolded, and simple laws are thwarted, by lawmakers who make laws only for their gains.

I am confused.

As I seek answers to the many 'whys in my head.'

Why this, and why that.

Those were they many whys that blurred my thinking. Before and now.

YES, OUR ROOTS, OUR CHAINS

The source of our joy,
The home of hope and shelter,
And now our chain.

The pains we go through,
the doubts about leaving home,
Where we grew up,
One's a familiar place,

where love and family are the centre,
Where we share,
Where we smile, laugh and rejoice, and cry together,

Where one feels safe, surrounded with love,
Culture and beauty,
Sweet place to be,
If it is kept at home,
Where no brother betrays, cheat and extort,

You could give all to be home,
Yes, that place we call home,

We could run to and not scared,
Where it all began,
And where now our pain lies,

Our roots our joy and our pains.

Just want to express here that our roots, our homes, our countries, our pains. That place we call home and are proud to refer to as home is no longer home for many of us.

We all wonder, seeking for a place we could put our pains, past behind and look forward to a new home. A new home that is never easy to call home. That will be full of strangers, different culture, attitude and norms.

A home you are first seen as an intruder, as one coming to steal jobs and cause havoc. Anywhere you go, you are at first treated with 'Be careful warnings.'

I always like to tell people where I come from with pride, but, is our roots making us proud, or have we failed our roots, and are in chain!

WHEN ORIGINS BECOMES A MEMORY.

"Home is that youthful region where a child is the only real living inhabitant. Parents, siblings, and neighbours, are mysterious apparitions, who come, go, and do strange, unfathomable things in and around the child, the regions only enfranchised citizen."

- Maya Angelou.

As the old saying goes, the two gifts we should give our children are our roots and wings. The roots will help them stay grounded in where they come from, and the wings will help them to fly and navigate the complications of life as they grow.

The worst thing happening is when it becomes too difficult to take your children home. Our root is all we have. For me, nothing can be compared to our root, it is holy, a beautiful, stronghold to build up future, and give identity, to be fully represented and recall history.

Whatever the scars of our roots,
the struggles and the pains.
Its nobility remains,

We may pretend and go about as if nothing happened,
 Roots are anchors,
Very unique,
And forms the hold of our heritage,

The gives foundation, and branch out
We may pretend not to know more of its value,
We may forget what it holds for us,
And destroy in greed, all we call root,

Where else do you want to reroute
even when you run far far away,
every thought will lead you back home,
Home where it all started,
And where we all hope to end!

We are hoping to take our children home, back to the root where we call home and origin. It is not only a matter of going abroad and establishing there. Yes, you could call anywhere home. But we will always long for home, where our hearts lie.

We are stuck in our ailing nation, our deplorable and corrupt nation, that we all are guilty of. We are strangulated and hang, immersed by our chains. We are soiled and incapacitated by the greed of wanting, acquiring and not distributing equally.

Are we surprised to see our nation ailing?

To see our wards run away, away from home,

It is no surprise to see China coming in again, our leaders are selling the remains, and playing political warfare.

A stage of drama,

A game of the throne,

Survival of the fittest.

Corruption stand in the way of our national integration, defectiveness of power tussle, watered by few rich ones, fuelled by power

Who will bail the cat?

THE NEED TO BE HOME

You are not supposed to be away from home,

You should be there to cheer and share,

But, who do you share your thoughts with?

I would have bet anything as I was growing up in a remote village of Mbaise that I would give anything to grow old there.

Despite leaving home a long time ago, my heart is there, in Nigeria. I carry my identity wherever I go. In my heart of hearts, I have never truly left home. I love my birthplace; however, I am not truly sure, it is what it was when I lived there and that I would fit in.

We never had enough then, but we had a real home — warm, painted with love and natural beauty. When you call a place a home, it means a shelter from all sorts of storm, and hardship-from all kinds of evil, danger and intimidations.

Something is going on today, a kind of feeling I am having and want to share with you. I am honest, and I write this because I love home, and that is why I am writing my feeling down to help me deal with the nostalgia that goes with these strange feelings.

SUDDENLY A STRANGER

We suddenly turned strangers in our homes,
We suddenly turned,
maybe, we will never have our root
the way we know it,
Things have changed,
Change changed and changes.

Some towns look like ghost cities,
As some faces say it all,

In the past it held hopes,
At present, it held despair,
resignation, tiredness and fatigue,

Yes, the faces say it all,
The aroma changed,
And the air is polluted,
Freedom ceased.

And eyes are constantly red as people are not the same again, even things that were very normal are not the same again.

What has changed?

A lot has changed, the people, the thinking, the leaders. In fact, everything changed and you suddenly, have these strange feelings, that it is never the same again.

Many times I try to dislodge this feeling, this melancholic feeling and dwell my thoughts on the past, and hopes.

Are we going to start looking for a home, when we think we already have one?

In the past, coming home was fun, and made the world more beautiful. But today, coming home is strange, because those feelings were no more.

Everyone has suddenly turned strange,

Those abroad have woken up to realise…ehhhh! You cannot even go home without protections!

Your close person is suddenly acting strange. If you cannot trust your root, where else can you be safe?

It is like a conspiracy of the time,

From those we share our thoughts and trusted. The system will milk you, sap you with no conscience.

Haba… Is all hardship?

The hardship that has robbed us of our innocence and turn us brutal against one another.

Hardship has taken the feelings of trust, love, sincerity and wisdom away from us.

Can we stick together again? And fight our fights together as one, and work our beautiful country to its natural beauty again?

Our forefathers made it together. Stuck together and played brother's keeper roles

Mhhhhhh!

Can we?

I asked me!

Stick together?

Shall we?

What need, what use!

In an age that hates each other. That speak lies and spread rumours. Wisdom has eluded us, togetherness has left us.

All we have is the shadow of the past, to memory that lingered,

Clamouring around us, near and cannot be reached again!

Alas, all have suddenly turned strange.

And we are suddenly strange in a newly made strange root.

CHAPTER 2: OUR ANCHOR

WHERE DO WE CALL HOME?

"I believe that one can never leave home. I believe that one carries the shadows, the dreams, the fears, and the dragons of home under one's skin, at the extreme corners of one's eyes and possibly in the gristle of the earlobe."

- Maya Angelou.

Yes, like Maya Angelou rightly put it, we all carry our homes wherever we go, no matter how long we left our original homes.

We should have a home where we can run to when other homes cease to be home again for us, in short, when we run out of homes we should be able to run home, to that place we call our root, our homes.

But can we just run back home!

Call anywhere home, but nothing will be as home as where you started, born, and grew up. You may have all the beauties in your new home, but you will one day realise that each thought of home tears you apart inside of that loving heart.

I am saddened, broken with thoughts and prayers, with my full list of what I have tabled to God.

God do this for me, help my home, make it a home again, make my fatherland, my root worthy to live again.

My instinct tells me always about home.

I clamour and wrap my hand around my continent, my nation, I look up to God and ask; why has everything gone wrong?

Please God?

My beautiful land, my pride.

FEELING NOSTALGIC

I miss my people, all I left at home. I love my country. Who will redeem us?

Who will be our Moses, Aaron, David, Joshua, etc.?

All are desperate in this time, desperate for everything other than change. Desperation to seek the impossible, without prayers.

In this difficult time, our desperation should be for positive change. With God for the attainment of impossible,

All might have gone wrong, pretty wrong, nonetheless let's shake heaven with our songs and prayers, for God's works are perfect. He is sure to be among us in these difficult times.

We can't get away without genuine prayers, we can't just walk out, without Him guiding us! Only Him can save! His day will surely come.

DO THEY CARE

If they don't care, we care.

If they don't want,

We care, we want,

If they don't preach love,

We do,

If they can't make us stand,

We stand,

When they attempt to destroy us,

We resist,

When they want us uprooted?
We resist,
When it gets so hard.
We work harder

Do they care,
No, they do not
We do.
Because we care?

They do not care; if they do, they will not mix leadership with emotion.

They would treat all equally irrespective of sex, religion, tribe, language, and so on.

Do they care?

If they did, we would be singing a different song

And loving and watering our roots,
We would handle all sacredly,
And not turn our land to a metaphorical battlefield
And let our wards run away and get drowned, slaughtered, sold, maltreated
Battered and beaten up,
In search of what they believe in,

Girls, women, boys, and men would be respected,
Animals would not take the place of humans,
Yes, if we all care,
Home will be home,
And not a scary place,
It will be a place for all,
No matter where you belong,
No matter the time of the year,
I would pick up my bag,

Dress my children up, and take them home,
No one would molest me,
And no one would scare me,
It will not be an imaginary home,

Made up in mind,
It will remain real,
and not imaginary existence,
will be full of love,
smiling faces,
and not men with guns,
yes, underworld men,
waiting to strike,

Do they care!
I do not know if they care
If they do,
They would have displayed good conscience,
Spoken the truth, and called a spade a spade,
Does the world care?
Am not sure they do,

Otherwise, their mirror would reflect nothing but the truth,

You see do they care,

No, they care for their gains,

they care for their gains,

They care to take and leave us doomed,

Do you know where many of the resources find their way?

Europe, America, or Asia. Even the money from the wealth of all, find their way in the hand of few corrupt politicians,

And the poor masses are left to struggle for 1 dollar a day.

You see! They don't care.

All states are broke,
Africa live in debt,

But do they care '?
You see no one cares,
Why don't we care for us!

For when we truly trust God,
Do the right things, press the right buttons?
Face reality, and remove sentiments,
God will remove the resource curse.
The paradox of plenty will be upturned and
utilised,
And everything will be right again,
And we all will be happy again,

Only when we become faithful and do our works
right, with fairness,

preach the good news and do the good part, and love our neighbours, when pastors and the ordained do it right, we all will do it perfect, and God will clean us inside out (Matthew 5.48).

YOUR DESPERATION

16 February 2019.

I love the book of Proverbs in the Holy Bible

The case of Solomon's story as a wise child that reflects the joy of being a good child who is said to be a pride of any family, as a bad child is seen as a shame. Our leaders are our pride when they lead well. No one should lead badly, so that you don't bring shame to your beloved country for treasures amassed in greed never last, and bring grief in the end.

The best way forward, is to do the right things as a leader, for it is good when leaders implement positive orders, that will bring a country forward and put things in their right places?

What good does it bring when we as a nation do wrong to our beloved nation, the land suffers, and the wards get chained, imprisoned and hopeless.

So why can't the leaders do the right thing? And let their people enjoy good leadership.

This is such a beautiful thing for any nation, for my beloved continent, how I wish that we will realise that "when the storm is over, the wicked is no more, but the upright stands firm forever" (Proverb10:25). I love Africa; I am so proud and passionate about Africa.

Who will not be proud of a beautiful root and colour?

That has nurtured many intellectuals and good people. I am grateful to Germany for giving me the stand to be who I am meant to be,

For giving me a home and shelter. For Africa, Nigeria, I am ever grateful for the root I share, and for giving me that which can never be taken away from me.

We all out here came from somewhere. We do not hate our roots; we only pray for our roots. We are all suffering from the wounds inflicted on us by our roots. I love my root so much as I suffer from time to time, the pains of seeing my root degenerate. One of the most difficult things for anyone is to leave all behind, to come in a very strange land where neither the culture nor the language looks similar. Where everything seems new, and where no matter the years spent, you will remain a stranger.

With this thought, I walk my lane alone, just to listen to the trees sing.

TREES SINGING

I walk my lane alone,
Watch the trees swing in all direction,
As the wind pushes them around,
I try to listen to know if trees sing,
Yes, they do,
Just walk alone,
Listen to the trees as they swing in the wind
Their leaves are telling some secrets.
Just listen,

As their bark sings songs of olden days,
 with their trunks that grow around.
Their roots give names and anchor lots,
This same song,
This same root, our root,
Sings,
Just listen, our roots sing too,
They can cry and scream,
When in pains,
Yes, our root, our chains,
Our Mother Nigeria screams in pains,
To see her children in chains,
And in exile.
 Yes, she is in pains.
 Just listen, our root is in pains
 And we are all in chains.

Inside us all, is this love of our roots, that give us a sense of who we are.

I wish all is going well in Nigeria. We have a beautiful culture, beautiful people and a blessed nation- But what is going on?

I know that election in Africa, especially in Nigeria, gives us nightmare, nonetheless this particular election 2019, gave us the widest fear of our lives.

I remember the 15th of Feb.2019, around 2 am, I was on night duty as a nurse, I suddenly had this news from FB the INEC chairman reporting that the presidential election was not going to hold again.

Gosh! I tried to reach home, could not get anyone to confirm the news as at that time. At the same time, I felt this panic grip me.

I got really scared because I thought just like every other Nigerians at home and abroad what could be going on. When we thought the election would come and gone, came this type of news that election was postponed. For us it means another long agony, waiting with mixed feelings.

To worsen it all, we got all sorts of reports about home on social media; I wept for my beloved country, I longed for the old times, the time of sanity, and tranquillity in all. I remembered my family.

I still remember the days when we were growing up. How happy we were and how free we felt about national issues.

Maybe there was corruption, and all manner of discriminations and crimes then, but we did not feel its strength, the way it is felt today.

Can you imagine most of us, being afraid to call home! Because you don't even know what you would be told.

I wept not because my country is not perfect; of course, I did not expect any perfection. I prayed for my people and for God to rescue my people.

I wept because of the degree of poverty that has plagued my beloved country, the recklessness of our youths and those we entrusted power on, how life has suddenly changed for many.

My heart broke in tears, and I became more scared. I immediately thought further on the future of my plan, and sudden fear gripped me," what are we going to tell our children. And what are we leaving behind for them".

I lingered, and dragged this question on,

But no answers.

CHAPTER 3:
RESCHEDULED ELECTIONS

Eventually, the news that followed was a reschedule of the election 2019 till 23rd Feb.; I did not know if I should cry or shout. This wasn't the kind of news most of us had hoped for.

This followed another sleepless night, agony and fears of our people at home. There were many questions, many whys to this sudden change. Well, nothing takes us unawares again. We are God's folks; He will not forget us

I quickly took my bible and turned to my consoling chapter (Isaiah, chapter 10:24-27).

TRUSTING IN GOD

That is why the Lord Yahweh Sabaoth say this:

> *My people who live in Zion,*
> *Do not be afraid of Assyria!*
> *He may strike you with the rod,*
> *He may raise the club against you*
> *(on the way from Egypt),*
> *but in a very short time*
> *the retribution will come to an end,*
> *and my anger will destroy them.*
>
> *Yahweh Sabaoth will brandish a whip at him,*
> *As He struck Midian at Oreb's Rock,*
> *Will brandish his rod at the Sea.*
>
> *As He raised it on the way from Egypt,*
> *When that day comes,*
> *His burden will fall from your shoulder,*

And His yoke from your neck,
And the yoke will be destroyed.

You may not understand this type of feelings except if you are from Nigeria. I hung on the phone throughout, looking out to hear the news that the elections were going well.

Towards evening we got messages that some parts were getting violent and, ballot votes were being burnt. God, I cried for mercy. Save my country. My root, a place I was born and grew up. I circulated for prayers, I beckoned all to go on their knees, and we continuously did a joint prayer. We heard that soldiers were designated to all villages, even to my village that used to be sacred, holy without violence.

I started calling from 5 pm on the day of the supposed election, to hear from those close to me that all was good. All the numbers I dialled, all were ringing, and no one picked. I started sending messages to our WhatsApp group, in the bid of hearing that all was well. Here I am it is 10.30 pm.

I got a short message that some areas were getting really violent, and some went peacefully. APC (All Progressive Congress), reports had it that some political parties were intimidating people, burning voter cards. This news spread around on social media, for example, in some part of Lagos, conflicts were reported. This kind of news made me sick and paralysed in my thoughts. We need God's interventions. I prayed and prayed, and it was this worrying thought that led to my writing this book.

I wrote my fears down, to present to God who saved the Israelites. My wish and hope is for a saviour from God.

I went back to read my Holy Bible, the old testament. The movement of the Israelites in Egypt in Exodus, I read it over and over again. Beginning from the time of the Israelites in Egypt, the prosperity of Hebrews, their oppression, the birth of Moses his escape to the land of Midian until when he went to see his Kinsmen as a grown up.

Moses did not forget the fact that he was a stranger in Midian. Yes, God remembered Israel, heard their groanings and remembered his covenant to Abraham, Isaac and Jacob.

Yes, as God sent Moses on this mission, he never told him it was going to be an easy journey.

The Israelites on their sides did not make life easy for Moses. Pharaoh, being stubborn, wanted to show his power.

But in the end, Moses and the Israelites sang the song of victory.

God, you are the strength of the oppressed,
The voice of the voiceless,
Father to the fatherless,
You are the God of Nigeria,
We shall live to worship you.
Holy is your name Lord,
Hear the cries of your children.

Redeem Nigeria and save her from anarchy and chaos,
We have sinned,
they said the would overtake,
But you alone is our refuge, our helper.
For You alone shall redeem Nigerians
Amen.

THE POWER TUSSLE

Is it an election of sorrow, bloodshed?

Why are we always struggling for power?

Nigerian election is always very violent. I am shocked to hear that about 73 candidates were contesting for the seat of presidency. This is not normal. President Buhari and PDP Atiku had better chances of winning, and their party dominated.

People's Democratic Party (PDP) and All Progressive Party (APC) were the strongest.

I heard parties everywhere were not best of friends during campaigns because everyone wants to win, but our case goes beyond, this is not maturity.

Most Nigerians are living in abject poverty. Many have to fight for just one poor meal a day. When one is sick and have no money, that is death penalty

Boko Haram in the North and Nigerians are running away to die either on their way to Europe through Libya, where they are maltreated, sold and tortured. Some take the risk of the boat to travel through the Mediterranean Sea only to die. Just very few of them made it to some part of Europe. This is not all about coming to Europe; it is all about running away from danger, hunger and poverty that have destroyed our roots.

Imagine our youths caught in various crimes, because of our broken roots. Don't fail to give people wings and teach them to fly.

How can this be explained?

Many African countries look unto Nigeria, but what do we have to offer in return?

Honestly speaking, I don't know which regime is better, and when a nation like Nigeria can overcome sentiments. Is Nigeria a myth a shadow of itself? – What has gone wrong with my country, are all our past glories gone?

Who will bail us?

Majority of Nigerians are suffering, and we are just banging on hopes.

You know the question is not who or what? but let us be honest, but I expected that the young politicians should be guided by the old ones, There is need to let the young ones also grow, and bring fresh innovation and vision, and try something new

It is not all about being a Muslim or a Christian. We should forget which religion is elected as a leader; rather we should pray to have a leader with vision and is capable of leading us out of Egypt and bringing us to that promise Land of Nigeria. Yes, the two contestants have served variously in the past –President Buhari leader at 76, a Muslim from Daura Niger state in the North, after being in the military in 1983 where he assisted late Brigadier Idiaghon as a vice. Late Brigadier Idiaghon the man that gave Nigerians a sense of discipline, fought corruption, and one would have said that was good for Nigeria then until suddenly Babangida took over in a silent coup. The questions for us are;

Who will lead us?

Who will be that Moses, Aaron or Joshua?

If we Nigerians should keep sentiments aside and think of a way forward, sure we will be on the right track again, Nigeria is too big, too populated and one can say Yes Atiku was then a vice president in 1999 till 2007.

Can he deliver when he is elected?

Nigerians are sceptical and are suspicious of all the parties, no matter who comes in now, one thing is that majority of Nigerians are simply tired.

Nigerians are desperate, tired, with not much of another alternative left.

Will Nigerians accept to keep aside selfishness for the sake of redeeming the lost image of our country?

I am really sad at the fate of our young generation, at the fact that our youths are just wasting, with no perspective in sight. I read Funmi Hammed, (June 6, 2018) article on, Nigerian Youth and Possible Solutions, they sought to understand the problems of the youths and suggested unemployment, laziness, bad Governance or corruption as major problems.

She stated poverty, lack of good health and many others as reasons. In all these are what I see as the major problems of our youths, bad governance and corruption because the other problems of the youths are rooted by bad governance that has little plans for the youth. Teach them how to fish, but unfortunately, the situation makes them fly without first learning to perch. This is bad for any nation, because the growth and progress of any nation, lies in how the youths are guided and prepared.

I think that Nigeria needs some fresh minds, and these fresh minds should be 'caught young' before they get polluted.

Why, why and why are we still hurting our roots?

People are disappointed and have lost faith in everything. Onnoghen Chief judge was arrested because of corruption according to the Guardian report.

The postponement of the election made Nigerians angrier; it is bad what is going on in Nigeria, as if the colonial masters would say, see them, they can't even rule themselves.

Don't we have some kind of remorse, shame as to what has become of our nation today?

Soldiers are to defend and ensure security; they are not meant to scare and take laws into their own hands. Our police today mmhhh! And one does not know who to turn to for protection, these are worrying.

OUR TEARS

Is it mere water running down the cheeks?

They are real tears, watering uncontrollably. Like raindrops, not ashamed of other eyes watching.

Yes, I am writing for millions,
who cannot shed their tears openly?
I am one of them, bruised in soul.
I am crying,
I cannot tell you how much I am hurt.

Leaving home,
Being away,
Yeah! Hearing of what has become of my root,
When all our neighbours' heads back home,
They do without fear.

We can't, for no safety is assured,
In a place, we have our roots,
Yes, I am so sad, deep down my root
Yes, I am crying for my beloved Nigeria,
My hope, my pride.

Who will understand our tears?
Our silent cries for our nation,
Yes, I know most will do,
Those whose roots are broken like mine.,
Those whose stem, trunk no longer supported

Their branches, and their leaves weird and are so fragile and wounded, bruised from its own people.

Who are busy struggling for power, and forget the tree on whose roots ensure continuity?

I don't think am the only one.
Obsessed about a nation, about my home,
That my beautiful small village in Mbaise
My home.

I call every day,
And my heart breaks at every call.
You know well that your people are in pains,
Are in fears and are hungry.
I ask why,
I beg why,

Deliver my people I murmur in tears.
My roots, my anchor! my pride,
My heart is with my people at home,
My roots! my home.
Saturday 23 February 2019.

Is it going to be another scandal again, vote of blood and intimidation?

We were not home, but we followed events online. The report of attacks gunfire in some areas, as voters find their way to elect a new president (Reported by Ruth Maclean, Eromo Ejejule in Lagos and Ismail from Maiduguri. Failure of technology and vote buying, doomed and loomed. Reports of people paying people up to 10,000 Naira just to get vote. They know people are hungry, but can you sell your freedom?

I followed and read their reports on-line even into early hours of Sunday. Na waoh, when will Nigeria learn the right way, these are worrying news especially when far away from home.

Yes, Nigeria has suffered under different leaders, is it bad luck or curse following Nigerians?

Reading about how Nigerians have chosen to pursue power at all cost, and fail to see that the nation Nigeria is in pains, of negligence.

What is INEC (Independent National Electoral Commission) doing and who occupied these seats. Postponing a voting by 5 hours to the election, this raised dust and made many Nigerians to recoil and ask themselves questions.

Reports of four people killed in Rivers State, Nigerian press, hundreds were on the run following the attack of Boko Haram in Yobeand this Islamic state West Africa Province (Nigerian Reporter).

Those in Maiduguri, Borno were reported being intimidated with gunfire, which was claimed not to be an attack (The Guardian)

What is going on, and will there ever be peace in Nigeria? Is it a curse? Or doom?

Atiku or President Buhari who will bale the cat?

Who will lead us?

Are we going to still prove to the world, and people like former Prime minister of Britain; that Nigeria is still fantastically corrupt, right?

Even up to ballot papers?

But this goes to this unceasing question of ", when are we going to learn to speak truth, to look at things in the face and call a spade a spade?

To stop ruling Nigeria with sentiments and emotion?

Religion and sentiment are not a solution.

When is Nigeria and its leaders going to think for a while about an average, poor Nigerian, and stop being selfish and stop thinking that Nigeria belongs to a particular group!

Are we a country of struggle or doom, this remained in my head?

Help us God to overcome. Late Martin Luther King led his people with this popular song. We shall overcome.

Will Nigeria ever overcome her predicament, corruption and hatred of one another?

Leaders especially African leaders keep on forgetting something.

When you serve your people well, they will serve you back. Help the masses they will make things easy for you.

WHO IS A LEADER?

*"A leader is one who knows the way,
goes the way, and shows the way."*

- John C. Maxwell.

This is such a beautiful quote for every leader

When leaders Do their works well, let their work speak for itself. When they start being realistic lead well people will follow.

I think most Africans believe being a president is like acquiring trophies, and getting titles, and amassing riches. This is very dangerous. No wonder everyone wants to be a leader.

73 presidential candidates, we read vying for the post of the president. I wonder what is in this seat that every Nigeria wants to put their ash on.

Is ruling an easy job? does it mean looking down and not upwards?

If it is that easy, why are other nations sailing, why do they have a fair judgement, and fair treatment?

Mmmmmm! But the said that uneasy lies the head that wears the crown? where are they heads!

Does this apply to ours?

Are they truly wearing the crown?

And are not feeling uneasy?

If so, whose crown are they wearing?

Igbos in Lagos we heard are tortured for exercising their voting rights,

and I ask again.

Are we a nation of what?

Why are we so power hungry, and reckless about Nigeria, our beloved root, that have provided us with everything? Why have we all sold our conscience, and no one is thinking how bruised our mother land is! How helpless and hopeless she is feeling, to watch what has become of her children, to see her children live in abject poverty, and with no hope for tomorrow,

Which mother can stand this pain,

This feelings of watching your own children run, and leave their roots in masses,

To hear every day the news that your own children took to flight to die in desert on their way to Libya,

To hear the deaths of many in Mediterranean Sea, crossing to Europe with a mere boat,

A boat of death and life.

How will you feel as a mother to be told in news that your many wards on flight for a better life are in prison in Libya?

And many sold out for organ trading,

In what is called modern 21st-century slave trade. That those dead are buried in mass grave, with no identity and no names on their graves. They are buried in a faraway home. Imagine the thought alone,

That your wards died lonely. This is just heart-broken. If you are a mother how will you feel. If she would be heard, she is screaming. None of us is hearing her.

She is in pains, and bleeding. Nonetheless, we cannot console her. Nigeria this message is for all of us.

Who will hear?

OUR MOTHER LAND

You speak and we do not hear,
You call and we do not answer,
You command and we do not obey,
How lucky are we,

to have you as a Mother,
full of resources.

Enough to feed all,
Oh! My mother's land,
What have we done, to warrant your wrath?
We weren't understanding your unspoken words.

Filled with motherly stuff,
And loving hands,
We have collectively failed you,
Woefully,
Do not let your wrath linger,
Even when you don't speak,
I feel your silence,
And I know that you are grieving,
And could burst in tears,
We are fortunate to have you,
So lucky to have all you acquired for us
Those natural resources,
Meant for all,

I see your face frowned in anger because we let
Them manipulate and control the wealth

You amassed for us and for our generations unborn,
Now, those masters have gone, but still have hold

Their motto is grab,
What they can't get,
The get through your wards that have,
Learned to milk you too

Truly, we have collectively let you down,
Weep not,
Do not abandon us,
Redeem your wards,
Mothers never leave their children,
For without you there won't be us.

CHAPTER 4:
WAITING FOR A MOSES

"Home is where one starts."

- T.S.Eliot.

Yes, like T S Eliot wrote, home is truly where we all start, and take off.

I cannot put it all into writing on what I call home. My sister art unleashed Dr. Vivian Timothy did so well in putting all into her artwork. This cover book, a beautiful artwork of Dr. Vivian, my sister reflects our motherland screaming, because of what has become of what we call home, where we started and where we hoped to end. Today We are left in good memory in paintings and in words of what home used to be for us.

You see when we feel this nostalgia about where we call home, we do these things to keep us going, and thinking good about home.

How can you forget where your journey began? Where you saw the first break light.

How could we not have thought of home before we destroyed her?

Home where we all have love in abundance, even when other material wealth lacks, home remains home.

I call it my magical home, because the old feelings bring me hopes and good feelings. I long to be there, to feel the atmosphere, the cold breeze, the birds singing early mornings and the cocks crowing to wake us up. The home where in the morning, you are woken up to sweep the compound, to make firewood, get dressed and dress for schools, Assignments done diligently, parents do their jobs, farming boomed and we were well fed.

Our smell of bricks of our houses, some thatched, but full of hopes and dreams. When am here I feel so good, because I know, yes am home?

The greatest when I am home, are my people, those who gave me love, and cared for me when Mama was not there. Even gave me food. We were good to one another, and felt loved from all,

Where will you compare to home?

Nowhere,

Yes, even when we have other homes, there is this feeling from the home you cannot uproot. Those things we did together feelings, going and walking into uncle's next-door house to say good morning, uncle in our native Igbo language. We pray for our homes, where we rooted, have roof and are protected.

THE PAIN FOR HOME GOES ON.

Home used to be the safest, no violence, and no fear. It scares to know that one will never find this home again.

Sometimes I feel no need, calling home,

Even when tempted to do so,

Still I would call because I would

not want to leave the lights die off,

Did not want to think it is over,

When I call home,

I hoped for better news.

Praying for better home,

home, my sweet home.

Don't know what it means to you?

Home is where I was born, grew up, got disciplined and loved.

Had my siblings, my play and peer groups, My family. Where we grew up in peace, harmony and love. Something very nostalgic about losing home.

A place you want to come back to, a place you carry in memory wherever you go,

A place that no other place can replace,

That is home.

We migrate to other places and try to make a home, yes, we make this home, good ones with struggles, but we can never make this original home to exists in a foreign land. Nothing bad, what is bad is when your original root is destroyed by those you trusted the most. Our leaders, our own people, those who were meant to support, protect us, when the turn wolf, you can forget that home will never be home again. They will scare and push you far far away from home, oh how we long to have our home again, our root, our nation.

It breaks my heart that nothing feels same again, everything changed, even the good smells are gone

I love my new home Germany,

However, it can't take the place of my original home,

I chase and discover my dream in Germany, nonetheless, I must go home to thank my home. To pay homage to where it all began, years back.

The feeling and the thought,
That you have a root,
twist smiles and brightens my face,
No place like home,
East, West, South and North, home is home
I know I will be seeing my people soon
That feeling of love, of reunion.

You will never walk home alone,
The beauty, the familiar feelings,
And the fact that you are not a stranger.

All exiles carry a map within them that points the way homeward.

Who will be our Moses?

Who will God send out from Midian to save our generation, and who will God send to accompany Moses and serve as a spokesman?

I bet everyone is asking this same question. I am so eager.

I listened to the INEC announcement on Facebook, all I wanted them to do was just announce the winner so that we will start working out on our head how to deal with the outcome of the election.

Yes, Nigeria has done a 2019 election, but who is the winner, and how clean was the process?

Yes, we saw and read all the things posted on the election, the things that goes with darkness. But this is Nigeria, of the 21st century, still accused of manipulating election. Have not gotten the reality and removed the sentiments, to just come out and choose who will move the nation forward.

What is really important for us?

It is not about sentiment of where one comes from, what religion, what language and how rich or influential, when is Nigeria going to learn from its mistakes. That it is not about, competition, not hatred, and not class.

I am so saddened, to read things, very negative, about what have become of home, of what is taking place in Nigeria at this 21st century Where is this going to take us to! sad, sad-

We need sober moments, to go into our shells and ask ourselves some real good and honest questions about what we are doing to our nation.

We are patient and have mastered terrible moments, and now hope and wait patiently for a real change and better life,

When will this happen?

OUR WISH FOR NIGERIA

Where there is no vision, the people perish - Proverbs 29:18.

Where is our vision? I have this feeling that got worst during this election. I do not want my country to sink into anarchy and perish, a country I love so much.

But what do we wish to make out of our Nigeria? We need our home, to rebuild, to restructure, or what do we want. We want a functioning nation, a place we could proudly call a home, where no one is neglected, equal rights, love and respect.

Yes, we have long endured the problem of tribalism, ethnocentric especially when it comes to choosing a representative, we rarely go for the right person, qualified and fit. We mix sentiment with reality and let our country suffer. We do this an end up losing our vision and remain year in year out, complaining and crying and still not ready for any change of any kind.

We cried and complained about the neo-colonial hold, now what is China doing with us again, going back the lane we have gone before

Can they make Nigeria function again?

As Victoria Moran, the author of Creating a charmed life said; Home is where the heart is. I may be disappointed with the happenings with the chaos we created, and with the way some politicians are running the country, still I cannot deny my root.

Because I care, I worry and I felt my only way of pouring out is putting down my pains in words and writings to appease my sleepless soul that have wondered and seek for answers about state of things with my beloved country. This book is my attempt to make sense of the woes of Nigeria, and I am looking at how many of us in the diaspora can contribute to the future of our country.

How we can put our brains together for the good of our beloved country, many out here have a lot to offer in rebuilding and restructuring, but the best we all can do is, by coming together and putting aside selfishness and work in one voice to save our country in despair.

Many of us have found a home in EU, America, Asia and elsewhere, we need to keep on helping, in sharing knowledge, impacting and inspiring one another, let's reach out and brainstorm to find a way out of this mess. Do not shy away in what you can do for the country. Do not close your eyes when things are not going well, join to speak out and condemn evil, for our root's worth securing and rebuilding.

If we destroy our roots, where else can we call home?

Don't be the only one fighting for change, because the problem of Nigeria is huge and needs collective efforts from home and abroad to bring a change.

We all are crying and complaining, but what have we done? And how may we come in, yes, we need every voice, for every voice count.

CHAPTER 5: OUR LEADERS

*We in the diaspora could
encourage our leaders, by proving we
can lead. What is delaying our leaders
from being leaders*

The resources should be used to create wealth for all, and add values that will keep our generation unborn.

Home is main the Seminary of all other institutions. Yes! our root, a public property, the foundation of states, the germs of the future man; and all that make the good citizen.

Where is this home!

It was as if our prayers and cries were not getting to God. I felt so terrible, so lonely and isolated thinking of home, my root as a chain that has been worsened by the feelings of the ongoing elections.

This is how I am feeling; I cried prayed fasted and hoped for just fairness in this 2019 election. Was it fair?

Mmmmhh. Are we Nigerians living according to God's law. I stumbled into the book of Leviticus 26 in the Holy Bible and read to the end.

I tried to reflect and even memorize this page. I know my God has never failed in His promises; the question is why he is failing us now. And is God so near but very far from my people. This filled my thoughts as the news on the election kept on reaching us.

Have we done so much to incur God's wrath?

Instead of peace, we are in chaos, like the land is full of beast and prey, and the enemies are pursuing the powerless. The enemies I prayed should be falling, but they are not falling, they are still pursuing.

Where is the God of Abraham, Isaac and Jacob? Who vowed to turn towards Nigerians? Uphold his covenant and make our land fertile, this I asked in silence and tears.

mmmm, where have we gone wrong and why have we not learnt to throw away bad behaviours that have caused us our national pride,

When are we prepared to give up the old and make way for positive change, where is our God that promised to be the God of many Nigerians? And the God of Imo state.

I begged Lord like millions of other Nigerians to fix our home.

Where is the God that brought the Israelites out of Egypt? We are in Egypt now, come and manifest your presence, and free us.

THE CURSES.

I came to the conclusion that we have being cursed, that we are invaded and infected and need heavenly healings. We have decided singly and collectively to put God's commandments behind and go astray. We have rejected God's laws and are worshipping power and money.

Now we are subjected and are consumed and gulped by curses we incurred on ourselves. God has turned against us, and we have succumbed instead of seeking God's face. They have a hold of us all, and now they have emerged.

We can't run again; we can't fly again.

Still we are not listening, this is our plague, our more punishment for our sins, will this reform and change us?

We are scattered, intimidated and bruised emotionally and physically. Most villages are laid desolate and are dry. Yes, fears have gotten hold, my people are powerless to even stand any threat. They are hungry and are just feeling dejected, deserted and abandoned, by our loving God.

The first time in many years, I felt this way, that we are being punished.

How else are my to explain what is going on in a country that I love so much?

I feel more nostalgic when I hear some of my friends from Kenya, Zambia, Zimbabwe travelling with ease home. I long to have my home back

Do you know how hard it is to make a home outside your original home?

To live a place you were born that is filled with love?

How does it feel to be exiled and feel alien in your home?

Is it like your home is burning?

I fight my tears back many times, as I visit my original home in memory the thought of peace and harmony that was experienced then, brought smiles back on my face,

But this is just an illusory, an imagination,

I carry this image everywhere I go, an image of a functioning country, an image of an ideal home, the way it should be, and the way it was

The one and only place and first place I called a country. The strongest ever. Nothing is better than feeling safe in your country, and nothing is as worst as being insecure in your home.

Whatever we do our country should be a secured place for homes, for foreign land still remain for us unknown,

No place can be like home, your country, but what if your country, ceases and deviates from what you know,

I listen to preachers, and I know from my feelings and experience that some things are not the same again. Recalling how lived those days together as families and as a united people, and seeing the picture of today. We never lived alone like trees, that are lonely, we lived collectively with our roots resting and rooted deeply, with love surrounding, to shelter and protect, represent, and defend us in danger.

Nothing is as good as having a beautiful country. When a country is let down by those meant to defend and protect it, the whole story is exposed, its sufferings, happiness, attacks, betrayal, storms.

Countries are foundations for homes, and whoever can rule well, listen and speak with their people, is a good leader, just watch trees, and you are watching human beings.

For man is nothing more than a growing tree.

For just like trees- whose strength lies in trust.

Men live and place their hands in leaders and expect to be led well. When their hopes are stricken, and they feel oppressed

They look unto a country with a good leadership. Where they hope to be smoothened and moved forward.

We crave good leadership with vision, we plan and focus, we will understand and lead them far.

When I think of what have become of my country.

It tears my heart,

I see my country rustle in the day and in the evenings,

When we stand, we doubt of what will be?

Can we imitate trees in their long thoughts, long breathings and wisdom?

To act wisely, and sing like them,

We will begin to understand so much,

And be like trees,

For trees are wise, only when we take time to listen to them sing,

HOW WE ARE RULED

It is not only a matter of winning, rather a matter of delivering. Without prejudice, hatred, and segregation.

How do we make it again?

Making home again, bringing not only memories, for new metaphors. Nevertheless finding that again which we left behind

Yes, election has come and gone on 23 February 2019, with the result after three days.

What happened in Senegal that conducted the election in one day and had the result same day. We are the giant of Africa, yes, we are.

What have we got to show that we are?

In the past, other countries trembled and respected the giant of Africa, today, unfortunately, our most beloved neighbouring countries are deporting our wards back to Nigeria at random.

Last month alone, over 750 Nigerians were deported from Ghana back to Nigeria.

What is happening that our past glory is disappeared?

Parents lead your children well, and your children will follow, leaders lead well, for no good leader have been known to have led alone.

Oh yes, what went behind closed doors, we will never be able to tell. Yes, we are the giant of Africa, my beloved country is no longer that giant that scared and respected.

Yes, I read it was a fair election, ok granted they were right, why the delay and why should people lose their lives?

> *"All of the great leaders have had*
> *on the characteristic in common: it*
> *was the willingness to confront*
> *unequivocally the major anxiety of*
> *their people in their time. This, and not*
> *much else, is the essence of leadership."*
>
> *- John Kenneth Galbraith.*

DEALING WITH THE MANY QUESTIONS

Have you read or watch the film "The GREEN MILES" (Film 1999) with Michael Clarke Duncan (John Coffey (Late 2012), Tom Hanks, Sam Rockwell, David Morse, Dough Hutson, James Cromwell, Michael Jeter and Bonnie Hunt, if not do so?

The character that made me shed tears was that of Michael Clarke accused of murder.

His death at 54 after suffering heart-attack devasted many as the expressed their sentiments about Duncan's passing away.

I am terribly saddened at the loss of Big Mike as he was called, Hanks, said in a statement to Entertainment. He was the treasure we all discovered on the set of The Green Mile. He was Magic. He was a big love of man, and his passing left many stunned.

Green Mile Director Frank Derbont speaking out described Duncan as the finest people he ever met and had the privilege to work with or know. He described late Duncan as the gentlest of souls – an exemplar of decency, integrity and kindness. Hearing this made me think why we can't even talk about our leaders in this way.

In another comment, Olivia Munn expressing her sadness wrote this. Michael Clarke Duncan always had a smile on his face and big hug ready for you.

While can't our land be ruled in this way, why can't this kind of legacy be left behind by the leaders?

Does anyone know why I choose the role of Late humble Michael Clarke Duncan ' in The Green Miles?

A literature film for this particular situation described in this book. In this film he was sentenced to death, because he was found with two dead bodies of two girls, he was totally misunderstood, and was accused, imprisoned and sentenced.

He was so special, and even in his naivety he worn hearts and had power to heal

He was presented as a very naive, childish and mentally handicapped black guy in the film who can only write his name.

He was innocent but could not get to convince the people because of racism; he got really tired with the injustice going on in the world and resigned to fate.

Is the injustice, discriminations, misjudgements not getting too much?

Have you imagined how many souls that have gone, languished, just because some groups hated their colour, their tribes, even their God?

Haba! when is this going to stop?

Ross-Perot once said this about leaders -Lead and inspire people. Don't try to manage and manipulate people. Inventories can be managed, but people must be led- are we not having the feelings that we are managed?

PERSEVERANCE

*'Sometimes you need to sit lonely
on the floor in a quiet room in order to
hear your own voice and not let it
drown in the noise of others'*

- Charlotte Eriksson-

On 9 March 2019, I stayed most of this day in solitary, in quietness and prayers.

The last time I travelled home, I found myself in doubt of what has become of my place. Broken and in shambles, potholes and, only God knows.

At this thought, whether Imo state will be good again, made chill ran through my system, and I became lonely and nostalgic, thinking of what it was in the past.

Owerri, in particular, used to be that dream capital, with the Owerri accent and that good feeling. I remember how important it feels telling people we went to Owerri. In those days people from the village will begin to look at you as if you went abroad, at mere mentioning Owerri.

What is Owerri again,

The aroma and the beauty gone,

What it was and what followed after…

Endurance they said is not the ability to bear a hard thing, but to turn hard thing into glory.

I wept in silence and longed for home

I wrote this for my beloved state, in memory of what it was and what it is now. Memory is beautiful in many ways and ugly in other ways. Whatever we do, we cannot do but remember the past.

IMO STATE

My pride,
My golden State,
And home of hope, peace and love,
What have become of you?
The state where I belong,
Where I have carried around with pride,
where one receives the heart of affection,
where once all were sweet, alive and bouncing,
perfume and aroma filled the cities,
and people slept in peace

And now this!

I urge you to never despair,
never relent, in seeking for your glory,
Show off your glory,
what you were known for.
Few years back,
You became Blurred and cut off,
stagnant and deprived
empty and void,
hungry and despair,

broken and trodden,
You cried and no one heard you,
you agitated but you were ignored,

Your quest for change lingered,
became louder and louder,
who will hear you,
and who will heal your wounds,
any right way to do this?
slowly, with mass prayers,
cries, down pour of tears,

May be everyone here knows,
We are the whole city,
and with God, we will rebuild,

We came close to where we belong,
Where we called home,
Our roots, our worries,
We will never lose the love to rebuild

To rearrange our inside,
and restore our emptiness,

today perfume your cities back,
replace collectively the stings, the fault scents
with the scents we knew before,

If we must pull together,
we must succeed together,
Work together and not be passive spectators,
We must not only hail names and cheer cheers,
We must perform our citizenship duties,
without fear

and have Imo State back again.

> *"This State will remain the state of*
> *the free only so long as it is the home of*
> *the brave"*

> *- Elmer Davis-*

I had wondered why we are blessed with all, and how some of us have ignored, and tormented the poor, force and inflict, and increased pounding hearts.

Wealth were amassed, and no splendour attached, haba!

This is not the state that we knew.

CHAPTER 6: WE GOT A MOSES

Source: Image courtesy of The Eastern Telegraph

I praised the Lord,
As the news got in the air
This good day, a good month, and good year,
Lord what would Imo State do without you?
For answering us, we will give back,
We will dance and sing,
Thank you for letting us do it,
For helping us persevere,
For telling us that we can do it.

We bless you,
We appreciate you,
For today we stand to sing praises,
To dance the dance of Esther and sing the songs
of praise,

We got depressed,
You lifted us,
And got us impressed,
We were down,
But you held us,
And showed us love,
Thank you, Lord,
We have hope again.

At last, at last, the news of Emeka Ihediohawinning the governorship election in Imo state came amidst of all odds on the 10 March 2019, this brought huge smiles and joy on the faces of Imo state people.

We all danced, cheered and praised God. He is the long-awaited Moses of Imo state. Now we pray that he will surround himself with good-minded people with visions, who will think positively for the good of the entire Imo people.

OUR NEW GOVERNOR

His Excellency, Rt. Hon Chief Sir Emeka Ihedioha, Nigerian politician and Businessman.

You are off to great place; today is your day. Your mountain is waiting, so get on your way.

Imo state suffered a great deal and setbacks in the past. It is not going to be easy for this incoming governor. I believe God; there are so many of us praying for Him, no evil shall come his way. He shall deliver, restore and rebuild Imo state with the people. He will remain the head, with his crown, and good will.

God is a God of the right time. We pray to God almighty that everyone should join hands together to help rebuild Imo state.

One love! Imo people. Together we shall make Imo state rise again.

We are going to say someday! If the world had more people like you, it would be a better place. You do make a difference

Few things in the world are more
powerful than a positive push. A smile.
A world of optimism and hope. You can
do it when things are tough.

- Richard DeVos.

Yes, our governor-elect, you can do it, govern well and people will follow. We believe in God. We trust He has sent us a Moses. A David to fight for us and defend us. I feel the zeal running in this governor-elect.

*To do the right thing. To work with those who
risked their lives to get things going,*

You got the tool,

To make your people feel important,

Not only you will succeed in leading,

You will be a good leader

*For we know that you are capable, strong, smart
and*

Have the love of your people and love of God.

It might look difficult, but you can

You have the courage.

Keep focus,

Remove negative thoughts,

work out positive results in your head,

But on your way are challenges,

You will pass failures by,

Face criticisms on your way to do the right thing,

Don't stay down, when it fails to work,

*Don't let them pull you down with negative words,
impatience,*

Every day may not be the best,

Always stay positive,

Perseverance, persistence and hard work will

Set things rolling.

The situation and the challenges will develop

Into a great leader

We are not expecting any perfect leader,

But you will do your best,

To inspire your people,

We will talk,

But what matters is your sunshine,

When Bonnie Blair said that; "winning doesn't always mean being first. Winning means you're doing better than you've done before."

Our governor-elect, we trust God that you will do your best.

GOVERNOR IHEDIOHA

Don't forget!

Like Orison Swett Marden rightly quoted that There is no investment one can make which will pay off so well as the effort to scatter sunshine and good cheer through one's establishment.

Governor-elect Emeka Ihedioha, we urge you to go scatter the sunshine with your charisma, and your goodwill for Imolites, for in the end you will be hailed and cheered.

Whoa, finally the day we all in Imo State had looked forward towards came finally.

And a Moses finally emerged.

This is the day the Lord has made for Imo People: We will rejoice and be glad in it- Psalm 118:249

Congratulations Imo State, Congratulations Governor-Elect

Thanks be to God, yes Imolites have made it, a leader has been elected, Glory to God.

.

FINAL WORDS:
TO MY READERS

"We are apt to love praise, but not deserve it. But if we would deserve it, we must love virtue more than that."

- William Penn.

I am not into politics, I am just merely a normal person, who is mourning the damage of my root, like many other Africans. Whose roots have been maimed, bruised and hurt? I am crying for justice, for peace, love and harmony. I am crying because of the loss of reality and the tussle for power and money.

I am not attached to any party, but to fairness, justice and equality irrespective of where one comes from, religion or language.

Yes, leadership and what it means to us Africans. We cherish and worship leadership, and make so much noise as we allow our voice to speak instead of our good action.

I think everyone especially the leaders should have to strive for the best.

Are our leaders doing the right thing?

"Leaders are made and not born; they are made by hard work, dedication and fairness. Guide and others will follow. In all, our greatest weakness is our emotion. We are short-sighted. Narrow-minded and blind in judgement.

Sometimes, I find it difficult to know who to blame, the few that are aspiring for power,

Or the few and many wanting to be used,

Yes, like a saying that goes.

Election is not and should not be a do or die matter. It should be fair, and should respect people's opinion.

When we allow truth, fairness and reality to guide us, we will go far. And we will find out that it is not about who wins an election, it is about who represents all equally.

Ultimately, leadership is not a crowing act, and not a mere celebration to show off. It's about keeping focused, having a vision and setting goal working and serving those who put you in power. Leaders should be motivated to do their best to achieve the best, especially when the stakes are high, and the consequences really matter. Leadership should mean making a state, or country to succeed and not helping a state to crumble.

It is not about APC, PDP and others,

It is about those masses, who are looking unto you. And not about any religion,

And not about any personal time to settle scores.

Let people trust you,

Listen to you,

Let them feel your help

Be your own mirror and be ready to step down, when they no longer trust you.

Force is not an answer it is a weakness,

and a sign of failure,
Make yourself that leader everyone wants to meet
When you visit,
Show them by your behaviour; leaders are leaders
and not dealer or negotiator?

Have you walked down the street to see that most roads are not passable,

Have you tried to send your sons and daughters to local schools to find out that there are no facilities and that poor families are not able to pay for their wards,

How about sending your children to normal universities, where sanitary and toiletries are in shamble, and parents struggle?

What about going to the hospital when your children get sick?

No drugs, no facilities,

Have you been hungry to know the value of a meal,

They are hungry; they are chased, no Agriculture, no good roads, no love and no peace,

They are all marginalised, monopolised, and segregated,

Sometimes you are in same country; you see some are more equal than the others,

I reflect on George Orwell's (1945) book" Animal Farm, Featuring Napoleon Bonaparte, Schneeball, Old Major, Schatzwutz, Boxer, Bauer Jones, An allegorical novel. According to Orwell, the fable reflects events leading up to Russian Revolution of 1917 and then on into Stalinist era of the Soviet Union.

Manor Farm run by Mr. Jones, a cruel drunkard. One day the wise old pig Mr Major was addressing the animals, calling them to rise up against the farmers, Snowbell led them, revolted and took over the farms from Mr Jones and changed the name to Animal Farm, with their 7 commandments with the most important stating that all animals are equal, four legs good, two legs bad.

The day Napoleon and Snowball fell out with each other, the saga continued with, following the battle of the windmill, see what happened to Boxer the horse and Napoleons friend, when he lost his strength, one would have expected some kind of special treatment from him, nope, he sent him to be slaughtered.

As the animals worked with men, they gradually developed the taste and style of men, and quickly changed the last commandment to " All animals are equal but some animals are more equal than others.

You know what happened, in this farm, some Animals were more equal, more important than the others. George Orwell was being sarcastic and come to think of it. Just see our world today as the world of " Animal farm of George Orwell

Yeah, there is anarchy, in the world.

Things have fallen apart- late Chinua Achebe would be saying in his grave. I warned you all, ahead. Yes, things have pretty fallen apart.

ACKNOWLEDGEMENTS

God renew our energy; we are tired. We all have accepted to keep our pains inside, because that is the safest place to hide pains and hidden tears. I wake up every morning to thank you Lord for another beautiful day.

We go through different journeys in life, as we all have to deal with different things in life. In my darkest moment in the past, I forgot my person, and became so lonely, frustrated and empty, and

I realised there is power in writing, in telling one's story. There were people who became very constant in my life and who made the journey worth going.

My Family

Thank you to my family that have always been there for me.

I am extremely thankful to my husband Hagen Meierdierks, and our bundle of joy, my daughter Shanaya.

To my parents-in-law Alfred and Christa. Tante Thea and Uncle Gerd.

My late parents Patrick Uzodinma and Elizabeth Adanma Uwazie, My siblings Adanne da Franca Uche and family, Da Ange Ndukwu, Chimeka and Family, Pauline Kanu and family, De Peter and De Cos and others.

The Professionals

I would like to show my gratitude to the professionals who helped me to make this book a success. They are;

Amina Chitembo of Diverse Cultures Publishing. Together with her team for making this book possible through the editing. Typesetting, and publishing this book even at short notice.

My sister Dr Vivian Timothy for always being willing to give a perfect painting for my cover books,

Thank you to my secondary school mate Editor and journalist Niche newspaper Iyke Amaechi whose brilliant updates of home kept me going during this election 2019.

Other Special People

Last but not by any means least thank you to those who have contributed to my Life:

Divas of Colour founder Mr Emeka and Faustina Anyanwu Thanks for the award as the best author 2018.

ABOUT ME, THE AUTHOR

My name is Clara Meierdierks (née Uwazie). I was born in Nnarambia Ahiara, Mbaise, Nigeria, to the late Mrs Elizabeth Adanma Nneoha Uwazie and the late Mr. Patrick Uzodinma Uwazie. My mother gave birth to eight children in total.

I am qualified as a Nurse/Midwife, a Quality Manager (Cert.) and have a B.Sc. (Hons) in Health and Social Welfare and an M.Sc. in Psychology. I am also a Respiratory Care Practitioner, as well as being a speaker, a blogger and an author. I am in my late 40s and just so happy that I have recently discovered why I was born. Being an author has added so much more colour into my life. I am so happy.

At the moment I am working with semi-coma and coma patients utilising life support aids, and I must confess that working with such patients has helped to reshape my life in a very positive way. These experiences have brought me closer to the realities of life.

I am very active in the field of women's organisations and empowerment. I am a founder member of CWO Bremen, and a member of the CWO at a national level. I am also an active member of 'African Week', an event which is held every year in Augsburg and where I have had the opportunity to speak on the causes of people having to take flight and immigration causes, and their likely solutions. My thanks go to my sister Vivian, Margret Aulbach, Julia Kupa and lots of others who have helped me in these matters.

I love reading and writing. I also love seeing people happy, and I pray that those I may have offended should forgive me. I do not hold anything against anyone, because it is a burden to do so, and I love my peace.

I believe that we all are born to be creative and no matter where we find ourselves, or the challenges we go through in life, we should not leave God, for through prayers we get our strength and faith, and through faith and hard work, the sky will be our starting point.

Just like any other person, I have gone through many challenges and have fallen many times. I just believe in never quitting - fight, pray, pursue your dreams, and the universe will do the rest.

PRAISE FOR THE BOOK

This is so brilliant and so amazing to produce such a book in such a short time. For those of us outside home could benefit in reading this book, to help heal the wounds of our roots.

We all are going about with different wounds incurred in us by our bad leaders. The only way to heal the wound is not only grumbling about a lost glory.

This book is well written and is short and compacted.

Thank you, Clara, for using your writing talent to help us deal with our various wounds.

Mrs. Franchesca Uche

COVER ART

〰〰〰〰〰〰〰〰〰〰〰〰〰〰〰〰〰〰〰

Artist: Dr Vivian Timothy- Art Unleashed
Painting Name: Self-Evolution Acrylic on Canvas
60/80cm
Website: Art-Unleashed.Com
Description: Prose Self-Evolution

Painting Myself Out of My Cage,
Liberating Myself From my fears and doubts,

Please! don't tell me I have arrived,

I am still on my journey to self,
Breaking free from the shackles of my past with
my Brush and colours.

Evolving as a person,
Still evolving,
Keep evolving."

BOOKS BY CLARA

C lara is a prolific writer, has written the following books published by Diverse Cultures Publishing. You can find the full collection of Clara's books on www.amazon.de or Amazon in your country or on her website: www. claram.net

Solo Books

The Long Struggle to Discovering Me

Published: 21 Nov. 2018
Paperback: 144 pages
Publisher: Diverse Cultures Publishing
Language: English
ISBN-13: 978-0995739611

Der lange Kampf mich selbst zu Fin-den

Published: 6 Jan. 2019
Paperback: 162 pages
Publisher: Diverse Cultures Publishing
Language: German
ISBN-13: 978-1916011403

Coming Out in May 2019

Our Root Our Chains:

Coping with the Nigerian Elections.
Language: English
ISBN: 978-1-9160114-4-1

YEARNING For A CHILD:

How to Deal with the Psychological Effects of Infertility and IVF.
Language: English
ISBN: 978-1-9160114-2-7

Co-Authored Books

Clara has contributed chapters in books including these books

Chapter Title: Maternal Bliss Delayed Not Denied
Book: The Perfect Migrant: how to achieve a Successful Life in Diaspora.
Paperback: 224 pages
Publisher: Diverse Cultures Publishing (27 May 2018)
Language: English
ISBN-13: 978-0995739697

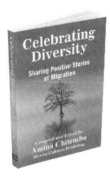

Chapter Title: PARENT-HOOD DIVERSITY
A letter to our special bundle of joy. Love you forever.
Book: Celebrating Diversity: Sharing Positive of Migration
Paperback: 220 pages
Publisher: Diverse Cultures Publishing (17 Oct. 2018)
Language: English
ISBN-13: 978-0995739680

Visit Clara's Website to Learn More and check
out the latest releases at:

www.claram.net

Printed in Great Britain
by Amazon